PISIFORM

A CONCISE TEXTBOOK OF UPPER LIMB ANATOMY FOR UNIVERSITY EXAMS

KARAN CHANDWANI | TANMAY SHARMA | VISHWAJEET CHARAN

ISBN 979-888629319-7

Dedicated

TO

Almighty God, Parents, Teachers, Family, Friends and well-wishers

- KARAN CHANDWANI, TANMAY SHARMA, VISHWAJEET CHARAN

Contents

Contents

वैष्णव जन तो तेने कहिये,
जे पीड परायी जाणे रे।

"He who understands the pain of others is one of God's own."

Foreword

I am extremely delighted and happy to know that the students of our college Jhalawar Medical College, Jhalawar , Rajasthan, India have came out with a book on upper limb anatomy for university exams. When they approached me with this different idea , Pisiform- A CONCISE TEXTBOOK OF UPPER LIMB ANATOMY FOR UNIVERSITY EXAMS, I readily welcomed this idea . This book covers gross upper limb anatomy , bones of upper limb and relevant radiographs . I hope this book will be useful for students to take a quick look before going for university exams.

I am using this opportunity to thank Karan Chandwani , Tanmay Sharma , Vishwajeet Charan of Third MBBS Part -1 (Batch 2019) , all staff members of Department of Anatomy and all those students of Jhalawar Medical College , Jhalawar who made it possible that this book can see the light of the day. I wish all the success for this venture.

(Dr. S.B. Sharma)
Dean
Jhalawar Medical College
Jhalawar

Preface

PISIFORM is intended to assist medical, dental, paramedical and nursing students to master the concepts of human anatomy essential to clinical care.

A recurring challenge in medical education is the common inability of the students to extract and memorize large factual information from the standard textbooks so there was a need for a book that can meet the needs of undergraduate medical students appearing for the exams, most of the information given is easy to compare and remember and clinical applications of the subject have been touched adequately.

We the authors have recently appeared for the First MBBS Main Examination, so we have faced the same fear during our university exams which gave us a spark to prepare such a book containing all the important and must to know topics for the university examination, in short, it is a final destination for all the last minute queries of UG students regarding the subject.

This book is not designed to challenge or replace any existing standard textbooks, but rather it is to be read as a companion text before appearing in the examination.

KARAN CHANDWANI
TANMAY SHARMA
VISHWAJEET CHARAN

Acknowledgements

When emotions are profound, words are sometimes not sufficient to express our thanks and gratitude. With these few words, we would like to thank our teachers at SRG Hospital and Jhalawar Medical College, Jhalawar Rajasthan for their exemplary guidance, motivation and constant encouragement throughout the course.

We are especially thankful to respected **Dr Shiv Bhagwan Sharma Sir (Dean, Jhalawar Medical College)** who gave us constant inspiration and support for writing this book.

We would like to acknowledge the encouragement and guidance of **Dr M.S. Rathore Sir (Professor and Head, Department of Anatomy), Dr Gopal Sharma Sir (Professor, Department of Anatomy), Dr Manoj Kumar Sharma Sir (Professor, Department of Anatomy), Dr Hemlata Sharma Ma'am (Associate Professor, Department of Anatomy) and Dr Varsha Porwal Ma'am (Demonstrator, Department of Anatomy)** in the completion of this book.

Although it is impossible to acknowledge the contribution of all individuals, we extend our heartfelt thanks to :

- Late Dr Atul Tiwari Sir (Former Professor and HOD, Department of Physiology)
- Dr Rajesh Agrawal Sir (Professor, Department of Physiology)
- Dr Shashikant Agrawal Sir (Professor, Department of Physiology)
- Dr Shrikant Shete Sir (Professor and HOD , Department of Physiology)
- Dr Ashwani Kumar Sir (Anatomy Faculty at DBMCI)
- Dr Ummed Singh Solanki Sir (Professor and HOD, Department of Biochemistry)
- Dr Ajay Kumar Bhargav Sir (Professor, Department of Biochemistry)
- Dr Chetna Jain Ma'am (Professor and HOD, Department of Pathology)
- Dr Rishi Diwan Sir (Professor, Department of Pathology)
- Dr Anshul Jhanwar Sir (Professor and HOD, Department of Pharmacology)
- Dr Tarun Vijayvargiya Sir (Professor, Department of Pharmacology)
- Dr Yogendra Kumar Tiwari Sir (Professor and HOD, Department of Microbiology)

We also take this opportunity to thank all of our friends, as without their support this book would not have been a complete one.

We would also like to express our deep gratitude to our parents, who have helped and supported us throughout the entire making process. And above all without the blessings of God Almighty, this book would not have been a complete one.

We would also like to take this opportunity to thank Sh. Mukesh Suwalka (Lab technician) and Sh. Sundar Lal Sen (D.H.A , Dept. of Anatomy) for helping us in capturing the images for our book.

KARAN CHANDWANI
TANMAY SHARMA
VISHWAJEET CHARAN

Rajasthan University Of Health Sciences
University Exam Paper - Blueprint

	MARKS	
THEORY		Two papers of 100 marks each (each paper shall have two sections i.e. Section A & Section B of 50 marks, respectively)
Paper I	100	
Paper II	100	
Practical + Viva (Oral)		
Practical	60	
Viva (Oral)	40	
	Total Marks = 300	
INTERNAL		Internal assessment marks are not to be added to marks of the University examinations and shall be shown separately in the grade card/mark sheet.
Theory	100	
Practical	100	

QUESTION PAPER TEMPLATE

FIRST MBBS UNIVERSITY EXAM

SUBJECT-: ANATOMY, PHYSIOLOGY, BIOCHEMISTRY; PAPER-I and PAPER-II

TIME: 3 HOURS

MAXIMUM MARKS:100

SECTION-A

Q.1 Fill in the blanks: (06 x 1 = 06 marks)

a.

b.

c.

d.

e.

f.

Q.2 Answer the following (04 x 1 = 04 marks)

a. Multiple choice question with four options

b. Multiple choice question with four options

c. Multiple choice question with four options

d. Multiple choice question with four options

Q.3 Clinical case study (15 marks)

(Give Clinical case description of one case with 3-5 questions)

Q.4 Write short notes on (Any five) (5x2=10 marks)

a.

b.

c.

d.

e.

f.

Q.5 Explain briefly (any three): (3x5=15 marks)

a.

b.

c.

d.

<u>SECTION B</u>

Q.6 Structured essay type question with clinical interpretation (20 marks)

Q.7 Write short notes on (any five) (5 X 2 = 10 marks)

OR

Explain Why (Any five)

a.

b.

c.

d.

e.

f.

Q.8 Explain briefly (any four): (4X5=20 marks)

a,b,c,d,e (5 sub parts)

Azadi Ka
Amrit Mahotsav

A Hidden Surprise

A small surprise for all of you from our side. A YouTube channel specially curated and created by the authors for you all. 100% free lectures for all the important topics of the 1st MBBS syllabus. Just scan the QR code given below to get access to free video lectures. In addition, you will also get a free online test at the end of that video which will help you assess what you have learnt so far.

References

- **Gray's anatomy: the anatomical basis of clinical practice**, Forty-first edition
- **Snell's Clinical Anatomy**, South Asian Edition
- **B D Chaurasia's Human Anatomy**, Eighth edition
- **Textbook of Anatomy: Upper Limb and Thorax**, Volume I, 2e Vishram Singh

CHAPTER ONE

MAMMARY GLAND

"The only limit to our realization of tomorrow will be our doubts today."
— Franklin Delano Roosevelt

MAMMARY GLAND

→ Modif^d SWEAT G

Loct^n

* Superf Fascia of Pectoral Region
* Axillary tail of Spence → Pierces deep F → "Foramen of Langer"
  → High % of Breast Tumor

Shape & Extent

* Hemispherical Buldge ; Vertically - II to VI Rib
  Horizontally - Sternum to mid-axill

Relations

* Pectoral F - Fascia covering Pectoralis Mj m/s
* 3 m/s - Pectoralis Mj
  Serratus Ant
  External Obliq

Structure

- Skin - Nipple & Areola
- Stroma - Connective Tissue & Fat → Bulk of Breast
  - Suspensory ligament of Cooper *
- Parenchyma - Milk secreting, 15-20 lobes, lobule
  - Acini, lactiferous duct & sinus

Blood Supply

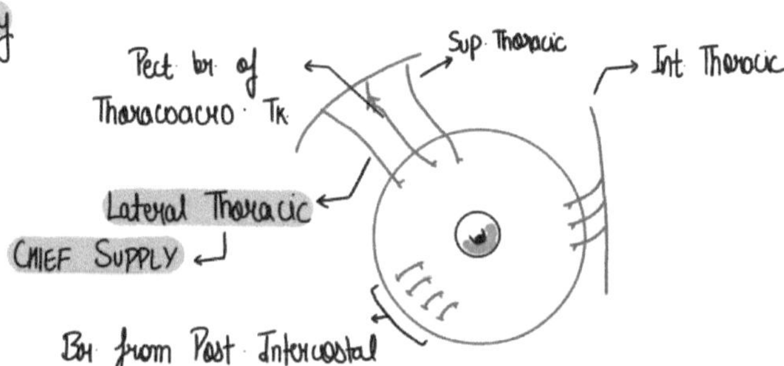

* Venous Drainage
  - Axillary v
  - Internal Thoracic v
  - Post Intercostal v

* Nerve Supply – T_2 – T_6 intercostal n/v (Ant + lat cutaneous)

Lymphatic Drainage

- Superf. → Skin (excpt Nipple & Areola)
- Deep → Nipple + Areola ⇓ * 'Subareolar Plexus of Sappey'

* Rest all Gland ↓

Most Common site of Breast Cancer

Malignancies move bilaterally Via communication of Sup. L.N.

All Ultimately drain to → Ant. Axillary

UL

UM

LL

LM

Internal Thoracic

Post. Intercostal

Sub-diphragmatic -peritoneal

Clinical

* Breast Cancer (♀ >>> ♂)
  - arises from epithelial cells of lactiferous ducts.

symptoms - Painless hard lump.
- Breast become fixed (mobility ↓)
- Skin Retraction, nipple retracted
- Pear d'orange appearance of skin.

* Kurkenberg's Tumor

Lower Medial ⟶ Sub-diphragmatic/Peritoneal ⟶ Ovary

CHAPTER TWO

CLAVIPECTORAL FASCIA

"You do not find the happy life. You make it."
— Camilla Eyring Kimball

CLAVIPECTORAL FASCIA

* Introduction
  - It is a strong shealth of fascia extending from pectoralis minor to inner surface of clavicle.

* Attachments
  - Medially, fuses with anterior intercostal membrane of upper two Intercostal spaces & attaches to 1st rib.
  - Laterally, Attaches to coracoid Process
  - Above, splits to enclose subclavius & attaches to subclavian grooves of clavicle.
  - Posteriorly, medial part fuses with deep cervical fascia, which connects the omohyoid to clavicle.
    , lateral part fuses with Axillary sheath
  - Below, splits to enclose pectoralis minor & ends laterally into short head of Biceps.

* Modifications – Costo coracoid ligament, Suspensory ligament of axilla.

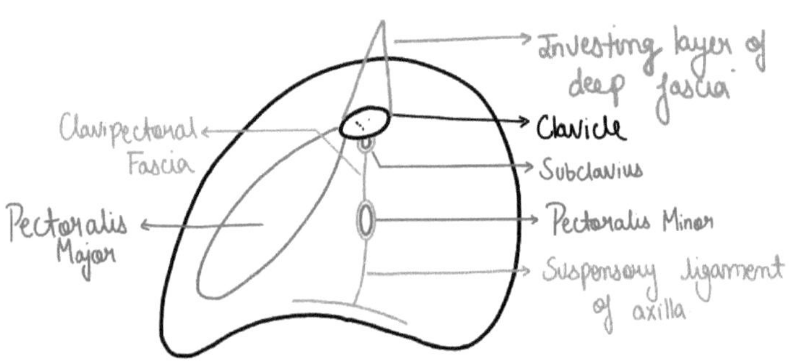

* Structure Piercing
  - Passing outwards – Thoracoacromian artery & branches
    - Lateral pectoral nerve
  - Passing inwards – Cephalic Vein
    - Lymphatic from Infraclavicular nodes

* Action – Maintain dome shape of axilla

* Applied – "Back Door Exit" for malignant cells of breast going to Reiters & apical group of lymph nodes.

CHAPTER THREE

AXILLA

"The power of imagination makes us infinite."
— John Muir

AXILLA (ARMPIT)

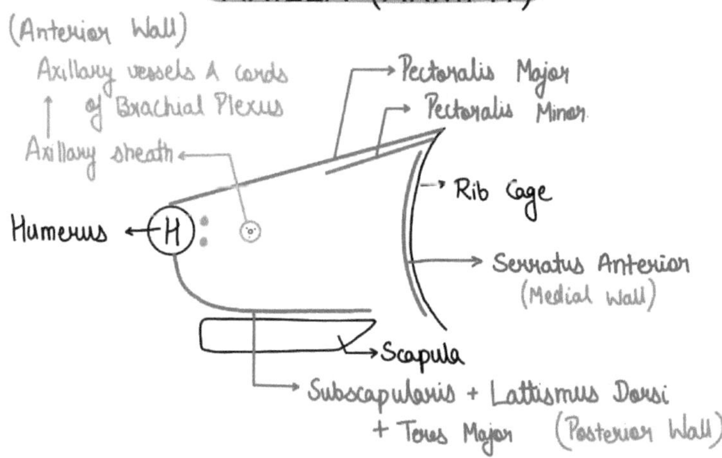

* Boundries & Walls

Apex – Medially, outer border of 1st Rib
– laterally, superior border of scapula
– Anteriorly, posterior border of clavicle

Base – Skin, Superficial fascia, Deep fascia

Anterior Wall – Superficial layer, Pectoralis Major
Deep layer, Pectoralis minor, Subclavius.

Posterior Wall – Subscapularis, Lattismus Dorsi, Teres Major

lateral Wall – Intertubercular sulcus of shaft of humerus which contain long head of biceps
– Short head of biceps

Medial Wall - Ribs & Intercostal muscles
- Serratus Anterior

* Contents
  - Axillary artery & its branches
  - Cords of brachial plexus
  - Axillary vein & its tributaries.
  - Axillary lymph nodes
  - Axillary fat

* Applied
  - Abscess in axilla may occur both superficial & deep to Pectoralis minor muscle.
  - Axillary abscess may be drained by putting incision at base of midway between anterior & posterior axillary folds.

CHAPTER FOUR

BRACHIAL PLEXUS

"You must not lose faith in humanity. Humanity is an ocean; if a few drops of the ocean are dirty, the ocean does not become dirty."
—Mahatma Gandhi

BRACHIAL PLEXUS

- Network of Nerve present at junction of neck & thorax
- formed by ventral primary rami of $C_5 - T_1$

* **Relations**

A) Supraclavicular part – Roots & Trunks lie above clavicle.
B) Retroclavicular part – Divisions of brachial plexus lie behind clavicle
C) Infraclavicular part – Cords & branches lie below clavicle

* **Branches.**

i) from roots – Dorsal Scapular nerve ⇒ supplies, Levator Scapulae Rhomboidus Major & Minor.
- Long Thoracic nerve ⇒ supplies Serratus Anterior

ii) from trunks – Suprascapular nerve ⇒ supplies, Supra & Infra spinatous shoulder joint, scapula.
- Nerve to Subclavius ⇒ supplies, Subclavius.

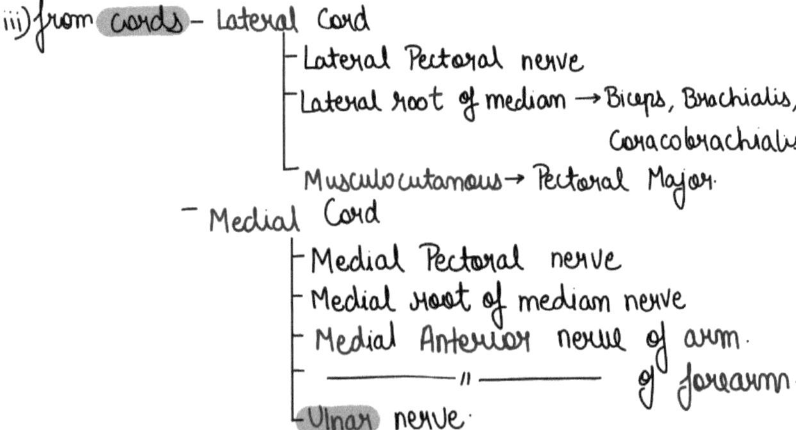

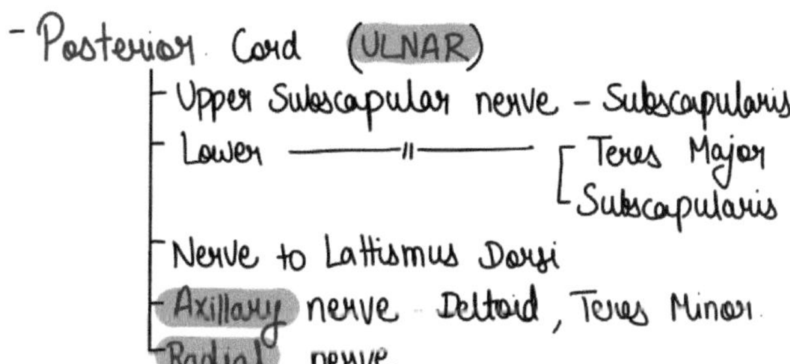

* Applied Anatomy.

A) Horner syndrome

- Involvement of sympathetic nerve, with T_1
- Usually occurs due to injury at root of brachial plexus.
- Hypohydrosis
- Ptosis.
- Narrow Palperable fissure.

B) Erb's Palsy —injury→ at Erb's Point.

Nerve involved.

- Ventral devision of V & VI cervical nerve.
- Suprascapular nerve.
- Nerve to subclavius
- Anterior & Posterior devision of Upper trunk.

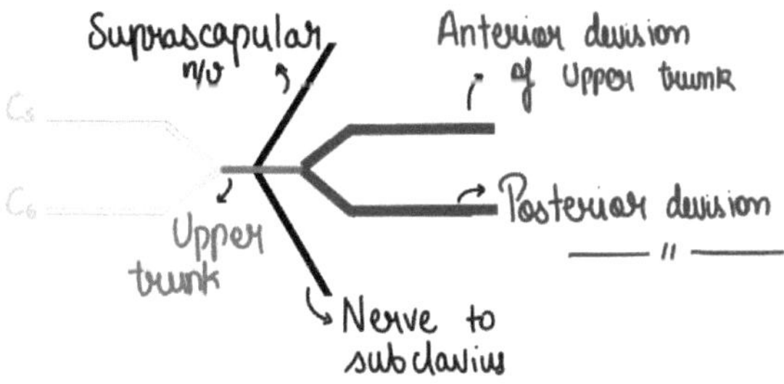

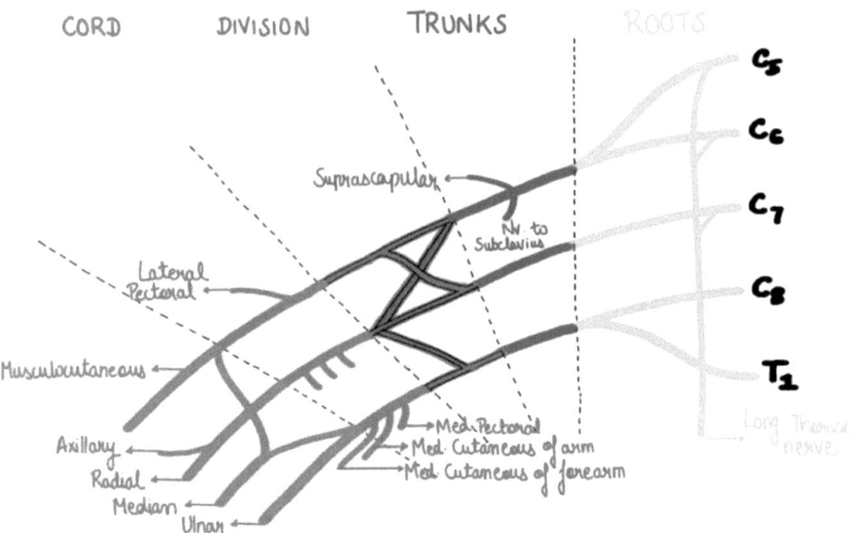
CORD
DIVISION
TRUNKS
ROOTS
C5
C6
C7
C8
T1
Suprascapular
Nv. to Subclavius
Lateral Pectoral
Musculocutaneous
Axillary
Radial
Median
Ulnar
Med. Pectoral
Med. Cutaneous of arm
Med. Cutaneous of forearm
Long Thoracic nerve

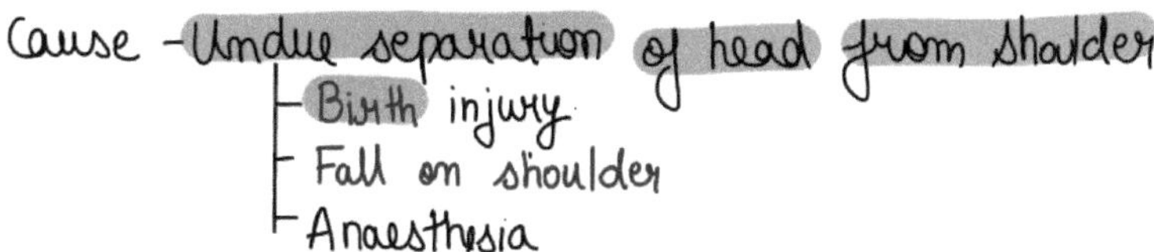

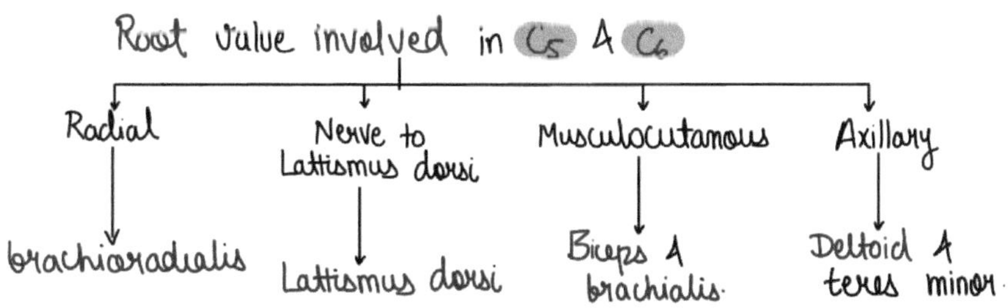

- Suprascapular = Supra & Infra - spinatus
- Upper & Lower Subscapular = Subscapularis & teres major

Clinical feature - Position of arm.
Hangs by side
Adducted
Medially rotated, forearm extended and pronoted

= aka Porter's tip hand
Waiter's tip hand
Policeman tip hand

C) Klumpke's
- Root value involved is $C_8 - T_1$
- Intrinsic muscles of hand involved

- Hyperextension at metacarpophalyngeal joint & flexion metaphalyngeal joint.
- cause CLAW HAND

CHAPTER FIVE

AXILLARY ARTERY

When you have a dream, you've got to grab it and never let go."
— Carol Burnett

AXILLARY ARTERY

Origin - Continuation of 3rd part Subclavian artery.

Extent - from outer border of 1st rib to lower border of teres major.

Relations - Axillary a. divided into 3 parts by Pectoralis minor muscle.

- 1st - Medial to P. minor.
- 2nd - Deep to P. minor.
- 3rd - Lateral to P. minor.

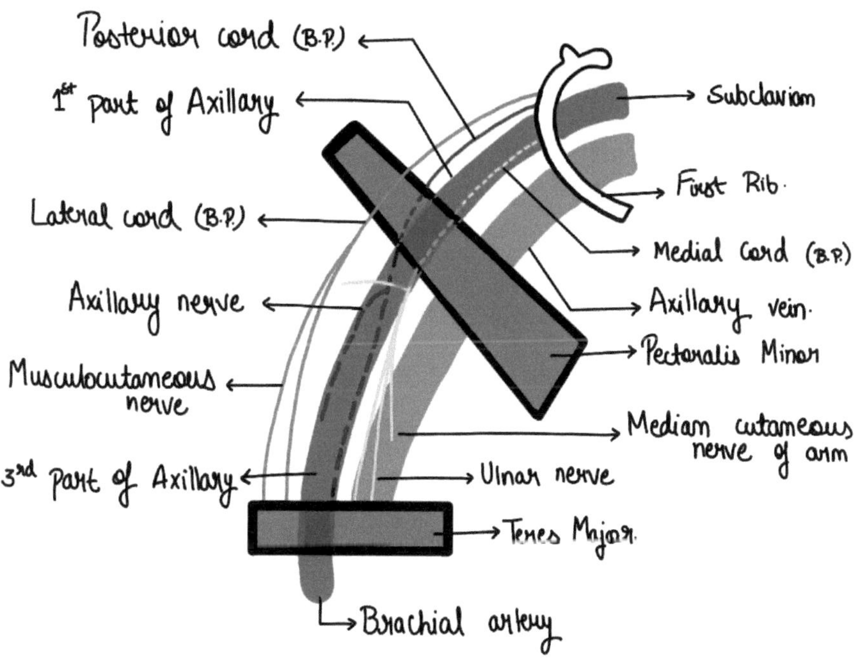

Part	Anterior	Posterior	Medial	Lateral
1st	– Skin, Superf fascia, Deep fascia, Platysma, Pect. minor.	• Medial cord of Brachial Plexus.	• Axillary vein	• Lateral & Posterior cord of Brachial Plx.
2nd	– Skin, Superf fascia, Deep fascia, Pect. major. Pect. minor.	• Posterior cord of brachial plx.	• Axillary vein, • Medial cord of brachial plx.	• Lateral cord of brachial plexus, • Coracobrachialis
3rd	– Skin, Superf fascia, Deep fascia, Pect. major.	• Upper & Lower subscapular nerve; • Nerve to Latt-ismus dorsi; • Axillary & Radial nerve.	• Axillary vein, • Medial cutenous nerve of arm & forearm. • Ulnar nerve.	• Carachobrachialis

Posterior circumflex Humeral a.
Anterior circumflex Humeral a.
Circumflex Humeral a.
Subscapular a.
A → Acromian
P → Pectoral
C → Clavicular
D → Deltoid
III
II
I
Superior thoracic a.
Pectoralis minor
Lateral thoracic a.

CHAPTER SIX

DELTOID MUSCLE

Don't judge each day by the harvest you reap but by the seeds that you plant.
-Robert Louis Stevenson

DELTOID MUSCLE

- Triangular, Multipinnate muscle, forming contour of shoulder.

fibres -	Anterior	Middle	Posterior
aka.	clavicular fibres	Acromian fibres	Scapular fibres.
origin	Ant. & upper surface of lat $1/3^{rd}$ of clavicle.	Lat. border of acromian process of scapula.	Lower lip of crest of spine of scapula.

insertion — DELTOID TUBEROSITY on HUMERUS

action	Flexion & Medial rotation at shoulder joint	strong abduction at shoulder joint	Extension & lateral rotation of shoulder joint

* Nerve Supply
- Axillary nerve = C_5 & C_6 of Posterior cord of Brachial plexus

* Structures under cover of deltoid –

(A) Bones = Upper end of humerus with greater & lesser tubercules, intertubercular sulcus, upper part of shaft & surgical neck of humerus.

= Coracoid process of scapula.

(B) Muscles, attached to—
- Greater tuber - Supra & Infra spinatous, teres minor
- Lesser tuber - Subscapularis
- Coracoid - origin of coracobrachialis & short head of biceps.
- Glenoid cavity - Long head of biceps & triceps

(C) Vessels = Anterior & Posterior circumflex humeral.
(D) Nerve = Axillary nerve.
(E) Joints & Ligaments = Shoulder joint & coracoacromian ligament.
(F) Bursae = Subacromian & Subdeltoid bursae & bursae of Shoulder joint

* Applied
- Fracture of surgical neck of humerus, cause lesion of axillary nerve, it results in Paralysis of deltoid. This affect movement of shoulder joint especially abduction from 15-90°.
- Paralysis of deltoid results with loss of rounded contour of shoulder.

CHAPTER SEVEN

INTERMUSCULAR SPACES

"Spread love everywhere you go."
— Mother Teresa

INTERMUSCULAR SPACE

Quadrangular space

* Boundries
    a) Above (Ant. ⟶ Post.)
        - Subscapularis (in front)
          Capsule of shoulder joint.
          Teres minor behind.
    b) Below - Teres Major
    c) Medial - Long head of triceps
    d) Lateral - Surgical neck of humerus.

* Structure passing
    - axillary nerve
    - Posterior circumflex Humeral vessels.

* Applied
    - Fracture in surgical neck of humerus Causes lesion in axillary nerve which lead to paralysis of Deltoid muscle.

Upper triangular space

* Boundries
    a) Above - Teres Minor
    b) Below - Teres Major
    c) Lateral - Long head of triceps
    d) Apex - Lateral border of scapula, where teres major & minor coverage

* Structure passing
    - Circumflex scapular artery

* Applied
    - Circumflex, scapular artery anastomose around scapula.

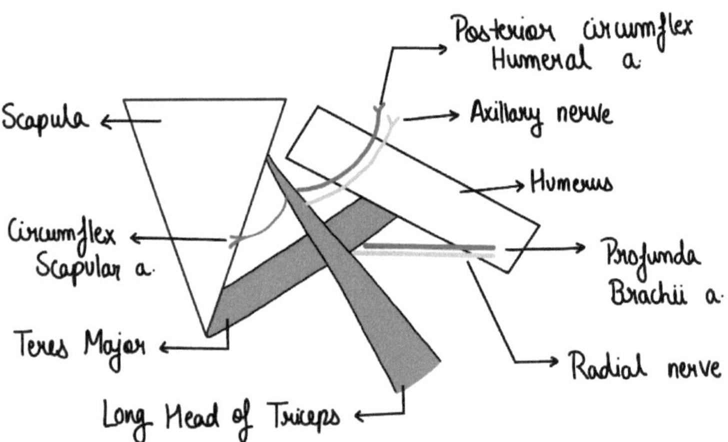

Lower Triangular space

* Boundries
    a) Above - Teres Major
    b) Lateral - Shaft of Humerus
    c) Medially - Long head of triceps.

* Structure passing
    - Radial nerve
    - Profunda brachii vessels.

* Applied
    - Fracture of middle third of humerus causes injury to radial nerve & lead to wrist drop.

CHAPTER EIGHT

BRACHIAL ARTERY

"You define your own life. Don't let other people write your script."
— Oprah Winfrey

BRACHIAL ARTERY

- Main artery of arm.
- Continuation of Axillary Artery, begins at lower border of teres mj. m/s.
- Terminals at the neck of radius by dividing into Radial & Ulnar ar.
- Superficial ar. [Brachial Pulse
  B.P. by Asultatory Method

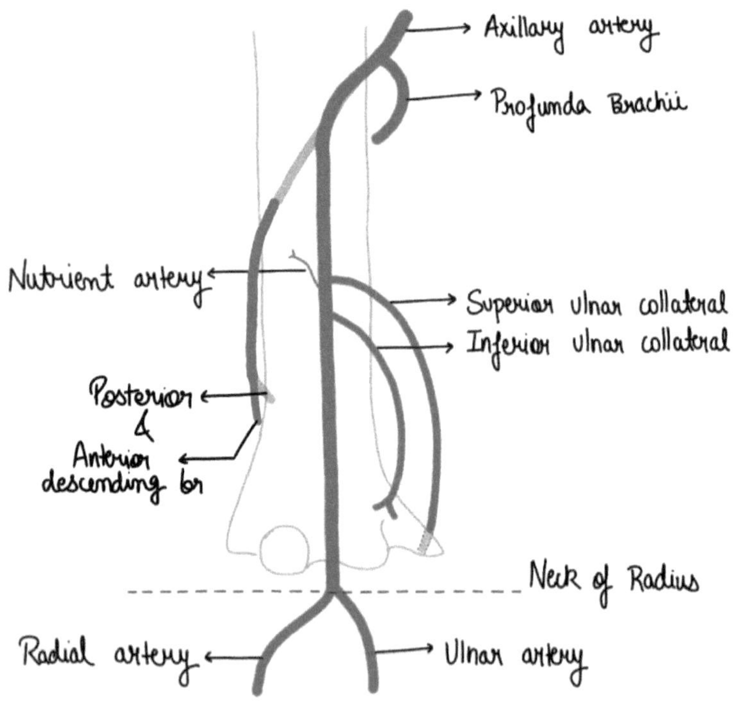

Enter Caption

CHAPTER NINE

CUBITAL FOSSA

"Don't be afraid. Because you're going to be afraid. But remember when you become afraid, just don't be afraid."
— Joan Jett

CUBITAL FOSSA

Boundries

Medial - Lateral border of Pronator teres

Lateral - Medial border of Brachioradialis.

Roof - formed by Skin & Superficial fascia containing

- Medial cutaneous nerve of forearm.
- Lateral cutaneous nerve of forearm.
- Medial cubital vein which is formed by Cephalic & Basilic vein

Floor
- Upper part = formed by lower part of brachialis.
- Lower part = formed by supinator.

Base - formed by an imaginary line joining medial & lateral epicondyle

Apex - formed by meeting point of brachioradialis & lateral border of pronator teres

Contents (Medial ⟶ Lateral)

mnemonic "MBBS"

- Median Nerve
- Brachial artery - (radial & ulnar too)
- Biceps tendon
- Superficial branch of Radial nerve.

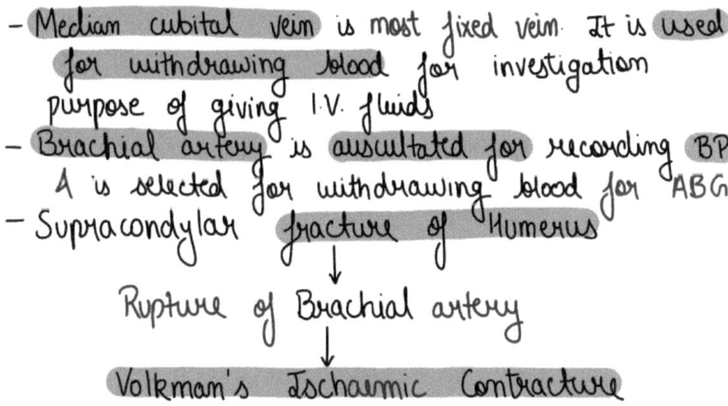
Applied
- Median cubital vein is most fixed vein. It is used for withdrawing blood for investigation purpose of giving I.V. fluids
- Brachial artery is auscultated for recording BP. A is selected for withdrawing blood for ABG
- Supracondylar fracture of Humerus
Rupture of Brachial artery
Volkman's Ischaemic Contracture

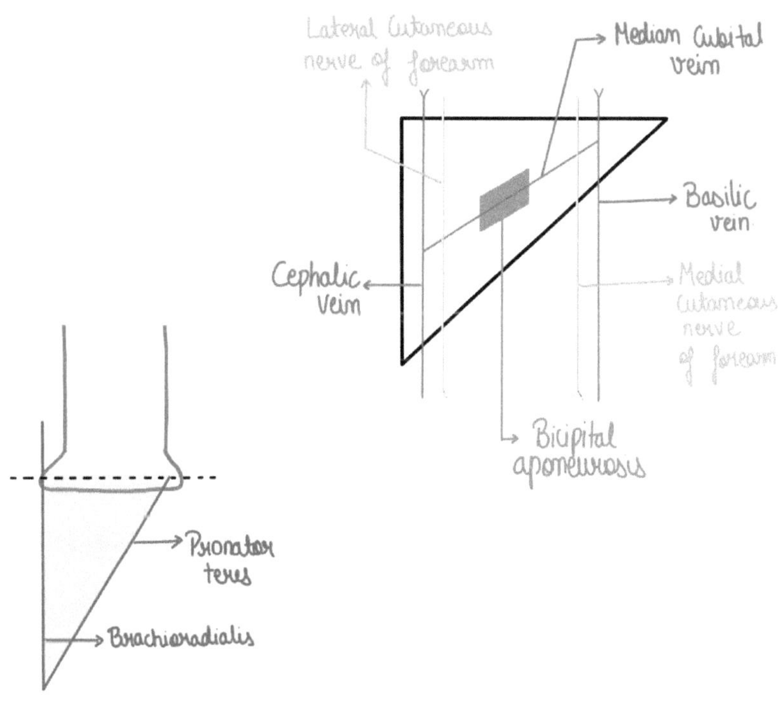
Lateral Cutaneous nerve of forearm
Median Cubital vein
Basilic vein
Cephalic Vein
Medial Cutaneous nerve of forearm
Bicipital aponeurosis
Pronator teres
Brachioradialis

Median Cubital Vein

* Origin from cephalic vein, & terminate in basilic vein,
  - it shunts blood from cephalic to basilic vein

* Relation - Skin & fascia
  Bicipital aponeurosis
  Brachial artery

  superficial → deep

* Applied - Used to withdraw blood for investigation.

Carrying Angle

* Introduction - Its is an angle formed by arm with forearm

* Reason - Medial flange of trochlea is 6mm which is lower than lateral flange.
  - Obliquity of Superior articular surface.

* Sex Difference - Not much difference between Male and Female

* Function - Helpfull in holding object

* Degree of angle - It is 163°c in fully extended elbow and supinated forearm
  - It is 0°c in full flexion & pronation of forearm.

CHAPTER TEN

ANATOMICAL SNUFF BOX

"I find that the harder I work, the more luck I seem to have."
—Thomas Jefferson

ANATOMICAL SNUFF BOX

* Elongated triangular depression on dorsum of hand in lateral aspect, seen when thumb is hyperextended

* Boundries -

Abbv.
APL - Abd. Polli. Longus
EPB - Ext. Polli Brevis
EPL - Ext. Polli Longus
ECRL - Ext. Carpi Radialis Longus
ECRB - Ext. Carpi Radialis Brevis

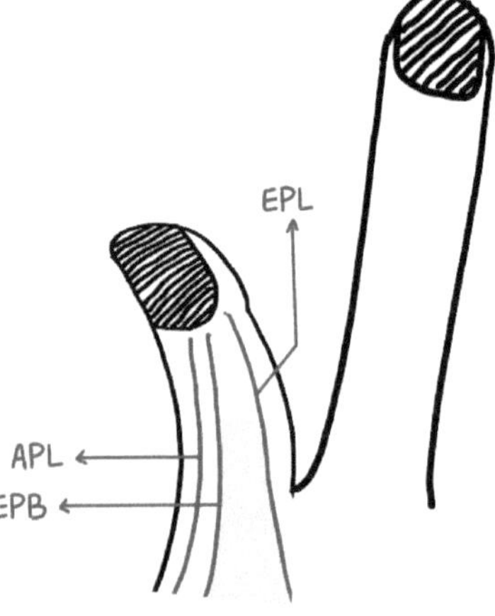

* Floor
  - Styloid Process (of radius)
  Scaphoid + Trapezium
  Base of I Meta-Carpal
  ECRL] - Tendons
  ECRB]

* Roof
  - Skin
  - Superf. fascia
  - Cephalic vein
  * Superf. br. of Radial nv.

* Content
  - Radial artery

CHAPTER ELEVEN

PALMAR ARCHES

"You are never too old to set another goal or to dream a new dream."
— Malala Yousafzai

PALMER ARCHES

Superficial Palmar Arches

- formed by ⇒ continution of Ulnar a. + completed by Superficial branch of Radial a.
- Lie distal to deep palmar arch

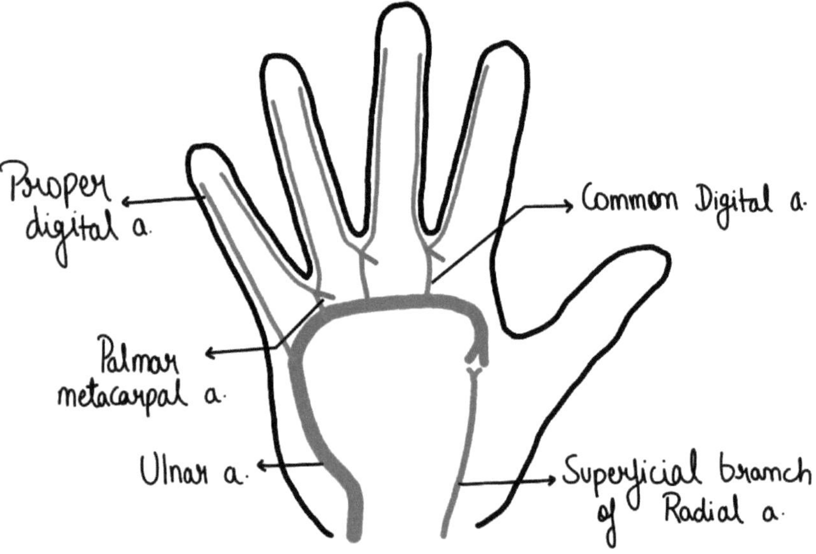

Branches - Proper digital a. - to little finger
- Three common digital a. - to 2nd, 3rd & 4th web. space.
- Cutaneous branches to Palm

Relations - Superf. - Palmar Aponeurosis.
- Deep - Muscles, Tendon of FDS, FDP, lumbricals

Deep Palmar Arches

- formed by ⇒ continution of Radial a. + completed by deep branch of Ulnar a.

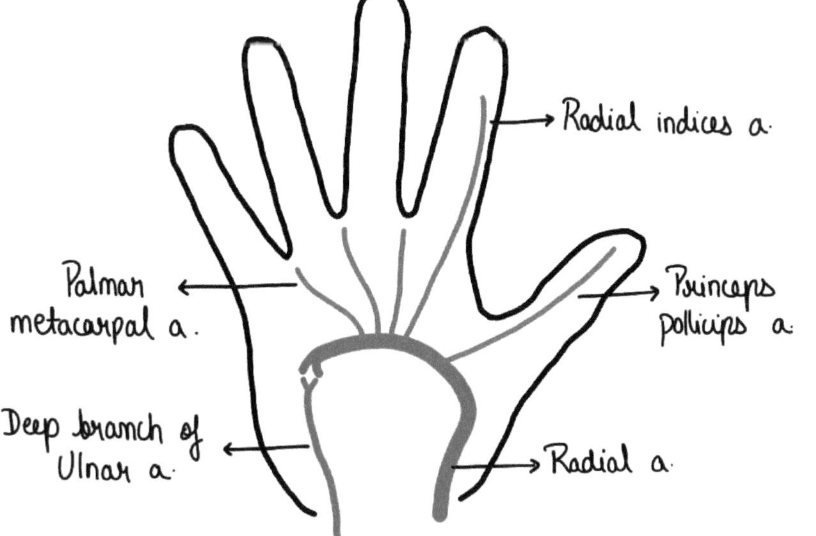

Branches - Princeps Pollices a.
- Radialis Indices a.
- Palmar- Metacarpal a. - Join common - digital arteries of Superficial Palmar arch.
- Three Perforating a. - 2nd to 4th Interosseous space
- Recurrent branch

Relations - Superf. - Muscles, Tendon of FDS + FDP lumbricals
- Deep - Metacarpal bones, Interosseous muscles,

CHAPTER TWELVE

IMPORTANT MUSCLES OF THE PECTORAL REGION

God answers in three ways:
He says 'YES' and gives you what you want.
He says 'NO' and gives you something better.
He says 'WAIT' and gives you the best.
-ANONYMOUS

IMPORTANT MUSCLES OF PECTORAL REGION

Pectoralis Mj.

	Origin	Insertion
Clavicular hd.	medial 1/2 of clavicle	lateral lip of Bicipital groove
Sternocostal hd.	lat. 1/2 of ant. sternum - II-IV Costal cart. - Ext. Oblq. Apo.	'U' shaped bilaminar tendon

* Nerve Supply :- Lateral + Medial Pectoral n/v

* Action :- Clavicular hd. - Flexion
Sternocostal hd. - Adduction A medial Rot^n

Serratus Ant.

Origin	Insertion
- Digitations from I-VIII Ribs	Costal Surface of Medial Scapular Border

* Nerve Supply :- Long Thoracic n/v / n/v to S.A. / n/v to Bell

* Action :- Boxer's m/s (scapular Border)
Overhead Abduction.

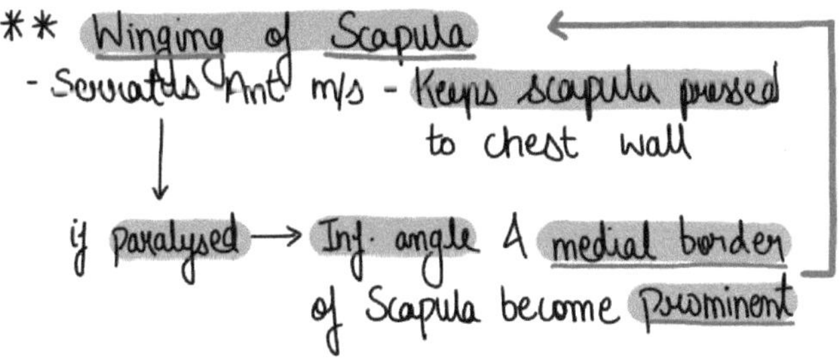

CHAPTER THIRTEEN

TRIANGLE OF AUSCULTATION

"People who succeed have momentum. The more they succeed, the more they want to succeed, and the more they find a way to succeed. Similarly, when someone is failing, the tendency is to get on a downward spiral that can even become a self-fulfilling prophecy."
-- Tony Robbins

TRIANGLE OF AUSCULTATION

- Small triangular space on back of trunk.
- Lies near the inferior angle of Scapula.
- Here, upper part of lower lobe of lung is present uncovered with any muscle. So, it can be easily auscultated by using a stethoscope

* Boundaries
- Upper border of lattisimus dorsi m/s
- Medial border of Scapula bone
- Inferolateral Br. of Trapezius m/s

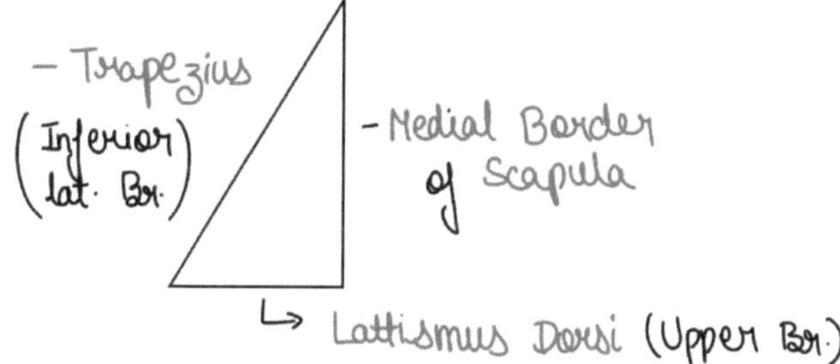

CHAPTER FOURTEEN

IMPORTANT MUSCLES OF BACK

"Success is walking from failure to failure with no loss of enthusiasm."
Winston Churchill

IMPORTANT MUSCLES OF BACK

Trapezius - Diamond Shape

Origin	Insertion
- Sup. Nauchal line	Clavicle (lat 1/3 Post. Br.)
- Ext. Occipital protuber.	Acromion Process
- Ligamentum Nuchae	Spine of Scapula
- Spine of C_7 to T_{12}	

* Nerve Supply :- Spinal Accessory (XI) n/v

* Action :- Elevate Scapula → SHRUGGING

- Retract —"— → BRING BACK
- Help in Overhead Abduction

Lattisimus Dorsi

Lattisimus ↓ WIDEST, Dorsi ↓ BACK

Origin	Insertion
- Spine of T_{1-12}	Floor of Bicipital groove on Humerus
- Thoraco-lumbar fascia	
- Inf. Scapular Angle	
- Post. of Iliac Crest	
- Lower 3-4 ribs.	

* Nerve Supply :- Thoraco-dorsal n/v from Posterior cord (Brachial Plx)

* Action :- Add., Ext. & medial rot^n of Humerus

- Climbing
- Forced expiration

CHAPTER FIFTEEN

SPACES IN HAND AND DUPUYTREN'S CONTRACTURE

"Don't limit yourself. Many people limit themselves to what they think they can do. You can go as far as your mind lets you. What you believe, remember, you can achieve."
—Mary Kay Ash

SPACES IN HAND

1) Thenar Space
2) Midpalmar Space
3) Pulp space in finger
4) Forearm space of Parona

- Thenar space communicates with fascial shealth of L_1
- Mid Palmar space communicates with fascial shealth of L_2, L_3, L_4
- Infection of Thenar Space are drained by inscising 1st web space
- Infection of midpalmar Space are drained by inscising 3rd & 4th web space
- Midpalmar Space communicate proximally to the "forearm space of parona" – space between FDP and FPL & Pronator Quadr
- Space of Parona extends proximally till oblique line of radius.

DUPUYTREN's CONTRACTURE

* Intro. – Its an Inflammation of ulnar side of palmar aponeurosis. There is thickening & contracture of palmar aponeurosis
* Causes – Due to fibrosis
* Features – Usually left hand is involved.
  - More severe towards ulnar side
  - There is more progressive flexion of 4th–5th digit
  - There is involvement of proximal & middle phalynx because of insertion of palmar aponeurosis.
  - A high correlation exists between Dupuytren contracture & CAD (coronary artery disease).

CHAPTER SIXTEEN

PULP SPACE

"If my mind can conceive it, if my heart can believe it, then I can achieve it."
— Muhammad Ali

PULP SPACE

- Space between skin and distal phalanges of all digits
- distal to fibrous sheath of flexor
- formed by fibrous septa. connecting skin to periosteum of distal phalynx.
- contents are subcutaneous fat & blood vessels.
- Blood supply of terminal phalynx by distal 4/5th part by digital arteries and proximal part by epiphyseal artery
- Applied = Infections in pulp space (of whitlow) can lead to avascular necrosis of distal 4/5th of distal phalynx.
  (base is spared because it is supplied by artery that is not in pulp space)
  = Abscess is drained by lateral incision and breaking all septa, In neglected cases may lead to avascular necrosis of terminal phalynx

CHAPTER SEVENTEEN

SHOULDER JOINT

"What lies behind you and what lies in front of you, pales in comparison to what lies inside of you."
— Ralph Waldo Emerson

SHOULDER/GLENOHUMERAL JOINT

* Classification - type, Simple, ball & socket, synovial joint

* Ligaments
  1) Capsule = attached to - of Humerus
  - tubercules & margins of glenoid cavity of scapula
  deficient at - bicipital groove
  - long head biceps
  strengthened by - spinatus muscles] rotator cuff
  - teres minor

  2) Glenoid labrum = fibrocartilage, in cross-section
  = functions - deepens shoulder cavity
  - protects edges of cavity
  - provides cushion to humerus

  3) Glenohumeral ligament = Condensation of part of capsule
  = Extends superiorly from superomedial margin of glenoid cavity

  4) Coracohumeral ligament
  5) Transverse humeral ligament.

* Movements
  Flexion - fibres of Deltoid
  - Pectoralis major
  Extension - fibres of deltoid
  - Lattismus Dorsi

Abduction - 0 to 10°] supraspinatous
10 - 15°]
15° - 90° deltoid
90° - 120° serratus anterior
120° - 180° serratus anterior (through shoulder girdle)

Adduction - Pectoralis Major
Lattismus Dorsi

Medial Rotation - Teres Major
Lattismus Dorsi
Pectoralis Major

Lateral Rotation - Teres minor
- Infraspinatus
- Deltoid

* Relations

Superiorly - Coracoacromian arch
- Subacromian bursae
- Suprasinatus

Inferiorly - Long head of triceps

Anteriorly - Subscapularis
- Coracobrachialis
- Short head of biceps

Posteriorly - Deltoid
- Infraspinatus
- Teres minor
- Long head biceps (Intracapsular)

* Blood Supply - Anterior & Posterior [illegible]
- Supra & Sub scapular artery

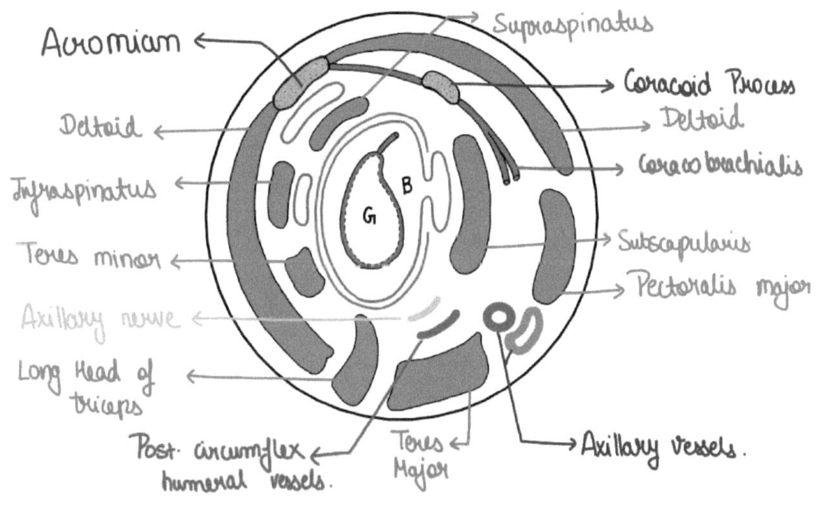

* Nerve Supply - Follow — Nerve supplying muscle also supply joint under, & skin over it'
    - Axillary nerve
    - Suprascapular
    - Musculocutaneous

* Applied - due to
    = disproportionate articular surface of head of humerus & glenoid cavity
    = laxity of capsule on inferior aspect

    - Frozen shoulder - due to adhesion between rotator cuff & humeral head, resulting into painfull & restricted movement

    - Shoulder tip pain - due to irritation of diaphragm, pain is referred to shoulder tip via C_3 & C_4 spinal segment

CHAPTER EIGHTEEN

STERNOCLAVICULAR JOINT

"I have not failed. I've just found 10,000 ways that won't work."
—Thomas A. Edison

STERNOCLAVICULAR JOINT

* Type - Synovial (Saddle variety)

* Articular surface
  - rounded sternal end of clavicle
  - superior socket at Manubrium sterni
  - 1st Costal Cartilage

* Articular disk
  - Fibrocartilagenous [super. - clavicle (medial hd.) ; infr. - I costal cartilage.
  - Strengthens Joint

* Articular capsule - attached to margins of the articular surfaces & articular disk.

* Ligaments
  - Interclavicular lig.
  - Sternoclavicular lig. (Ant & Post.)
  - Costoclavicular lig.

* Importance
  - In weight transmission from upper limb to axial skelton.
  - Allows movement of pectoral girdle.

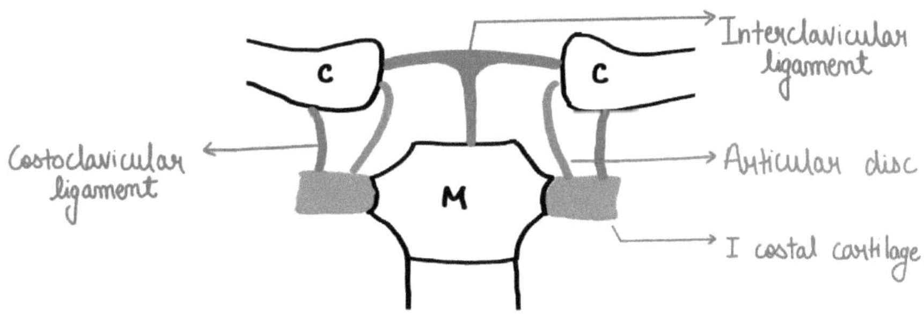

CHAPTER NINETEEN

RADIAL NERVE

"One day or day one. You decide."

RADIAL NERVE

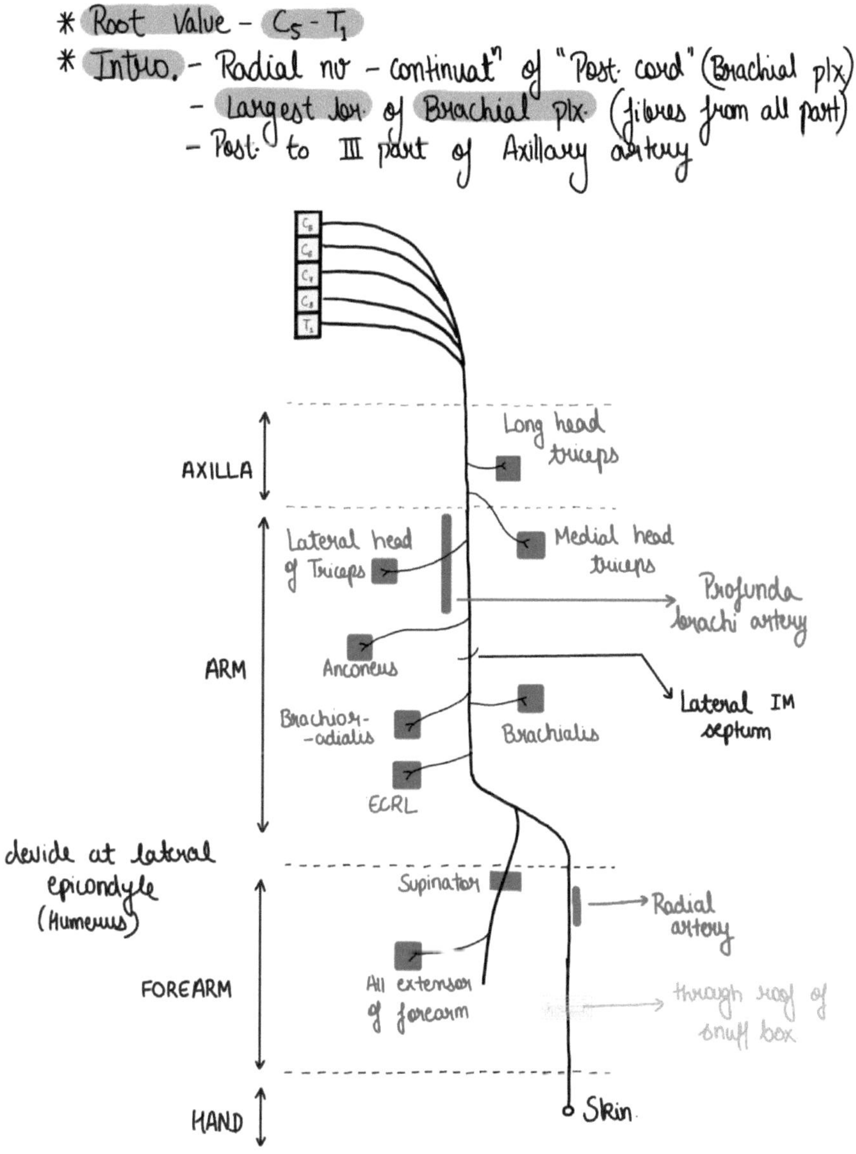

* Cutaneous / Sensory Supply
  - Posterior arm + Forearm
  - Dorsum of hand (Lateral ½) + Lateral 3½ digits on dorsum.

* Clinical Corelation

I) Axilla → Crutch Paralysis - due to the pressure of upper end of crutch.

c/f - loss of
- → extension
  - → elbow - Triceps #
  - → wrist - Wrist drop.
  - → digits
- → supination → in extended elbow
- → sensation → over complete area supplied by radial n/v

II) Arm (in radial groove)

Reasons
- Midshaft fracture of Humerus
- Wrongly placed IM injection
- Saturday night paralysis
  - drunkard falling asleep over the chair with its one arm at back of chair

c/f
- weakness in elbow extension - (long & med. head of triceps spared)
- Wrist drop.
- Loss of
  - → extension of fingers
  - → supination in extended elbow
  - → sensation in hand dorsum (becoz. cutanous n/v supplying arm & forearm are spared)

III) Elbow → Radial Tunnel Syndr. – entrapment of deep branch of radial n/v at elbow

Reasons – due to fibrous bands, compress n/v at radiohumeral joint
- Sharp margin of ECRB

c/f – Loss of Extension → wrist (NO WRIST DROP)
↳ digits
- Pain over the extensor aspect of forearm.
- Elbow extension – NORMAL

CHAPTER TWENTY

ULNAR NERVE

"Belief creates the actual fact."
— William James

ULNAR NERVE

* Root Value - $C_7 - T_1$
* Intro. - This nerve lies medial to III part of axillary artery.
  - also known as Musician nerve / nerve of fine movements
  - Lies behind the medial epicondyle of humerus & is termed as Funny Bone
  - No branch in Axilla & Arm

** All Intrinsic muscles of hand are supplied by Ulnar except Thenar eminence & I, II Lumbricals

* Cutaneous / Sensory Supply - Medial 1/3 of Hand, Medial 1½ digits] Both aspect (Ant. + Post.)

* Clinical Corelation

I) Elbow - due to medial epicondyle fracture
- Compression b/w two heads of F.C.U

c/f - Atropy & flattening of Hypothenar eminence
- Claw hand : as it involves ring & little finger only
  - ↳ not complete claw hand.
    (occur when both median & Ulnar #)
- Loss of Abd. & Add. of fingers - Paralysis of intrinsic m/s of hand.
- Loss of Add. of thumb.
- Sensory loss - all over the area supplied

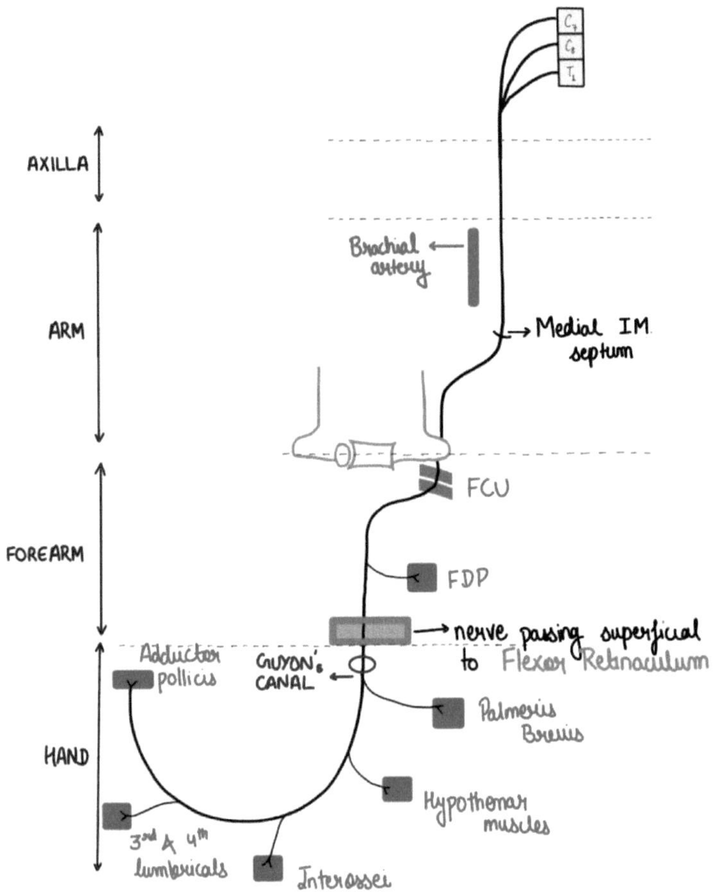

II) Wrist - due to compression in GUYON'S CANAL
- vulnerable to injury as it is superficial.

c/f - ULNAR PARADOX : Higher/Proximal the injury = less severe Claw hand

- Hypothenar eminence : Atrophy + Flattening
- Fingers : loss of Abduction & Adduction

CHAPTER TWENTY-ONE

MEDIAN NERVE

"Happiness is not something ready-made. It comes from your own actions."
— Dalai Lama XIV

MEDIAN NERVE

* Root Value – $C_5 - T_1$
* Intro. – arises from union of latr. & med. roots (Brachial plx)

* Relat^n
  - → Axilla – latr. to IIIrd part of Axillary artery
  - → Mid Humerus – crosses brachial a. from lat. to medial
  - → Cubital Fossa – medial most content.
  - → Enter forearm by piercing pronator teres

* Memory Aid – All the muscle of front of forearm are supplied by median n/v
  except → Flx. Carpi Ulnaris (FCU) & Med. 1/2 of Flx. Digit. Profond. (FDP)

* Cutaneous Supply – Lat. 2/3 of Palm of Hand,
  Lat. 3½ digits + Nail Beds

* Clinical Correlation –
  (I) Elbow – supracondylar fracture of Humerus
  c/f – Forearm in supine position
  - Wrist flexion is weak
  - Wrist – adducted
  - No flexion at IP joints of Index & Middle finger.
  - Sensory loss – Lateral ½ of Palm + Lateral 3½ + Nail beds

  - APE THUMB DEFORMITY – thenar eminence flattening
    – Thumb adducted (loss of opposition)

(II) Mid Forearm

c/f - Pointing index finger
- APE thumb deformity
- Loss of sensation

(III) Wrist

due to - deep laceration (suicidal cuts)

c/f - APE Thumb deformity.
- Loss of sensation

PLEASE TURN OVER

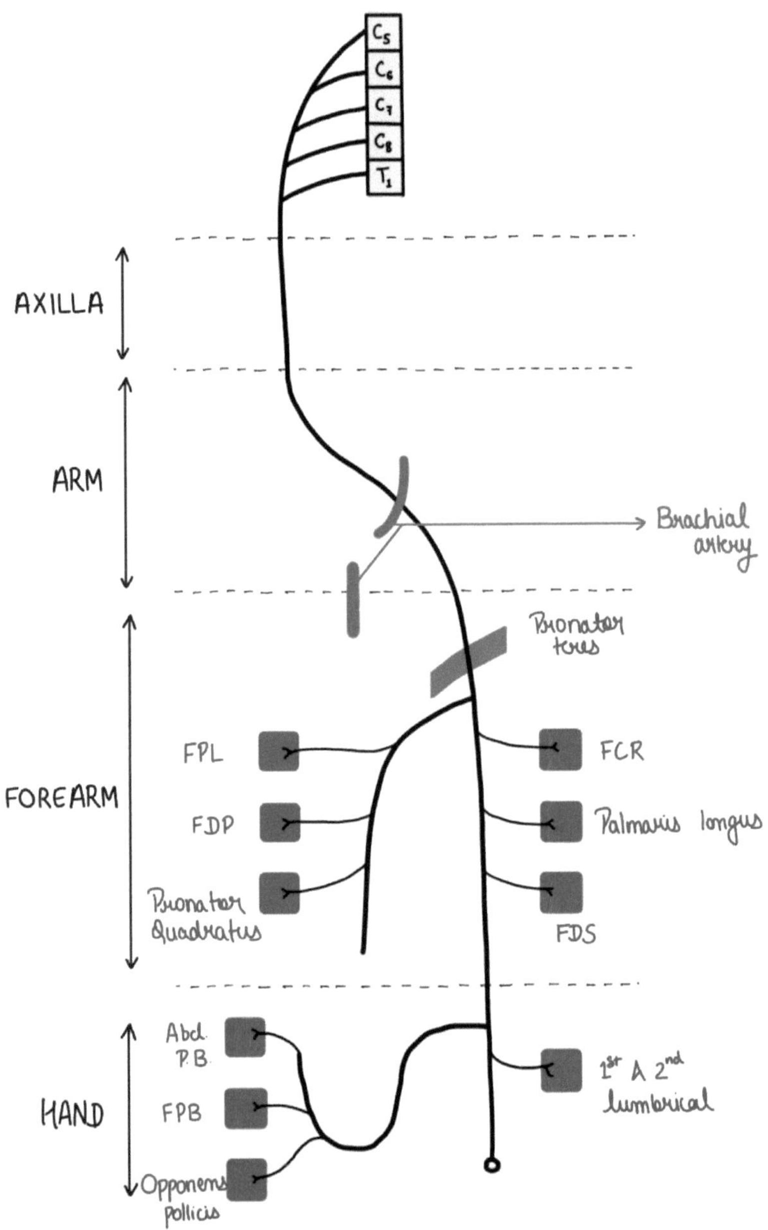
C5
C6
C7
C8
T1
AXILLA
ARM
Brachial artery
FOREARM
Pronator teres
FPL
FCR
FDP
Palmaris longus
Pronator Quadratus
FDS
HAND
Abd. P.B.
FPB
Opponens pollicis
1st & 2nd lumbrical

CHAPTER TWENTY-TWO

MUSCULOCUTANEOUS NERVE

"All progress takes place outside the comfort zone."
—Michael John Bobak

MUSCULOCUTANEOUS NERVE

* Origin & course
  - Arises from lateral cord of brachial Plx. C_{5-7}
  - Then pierce coracobrach. m/s & runs on Anterior aspect of Arm.
  - Runs in b/w Biceps & Brachialis
  - Then after cubital fossa it becomes lateral cutaneous nerve of forearm.

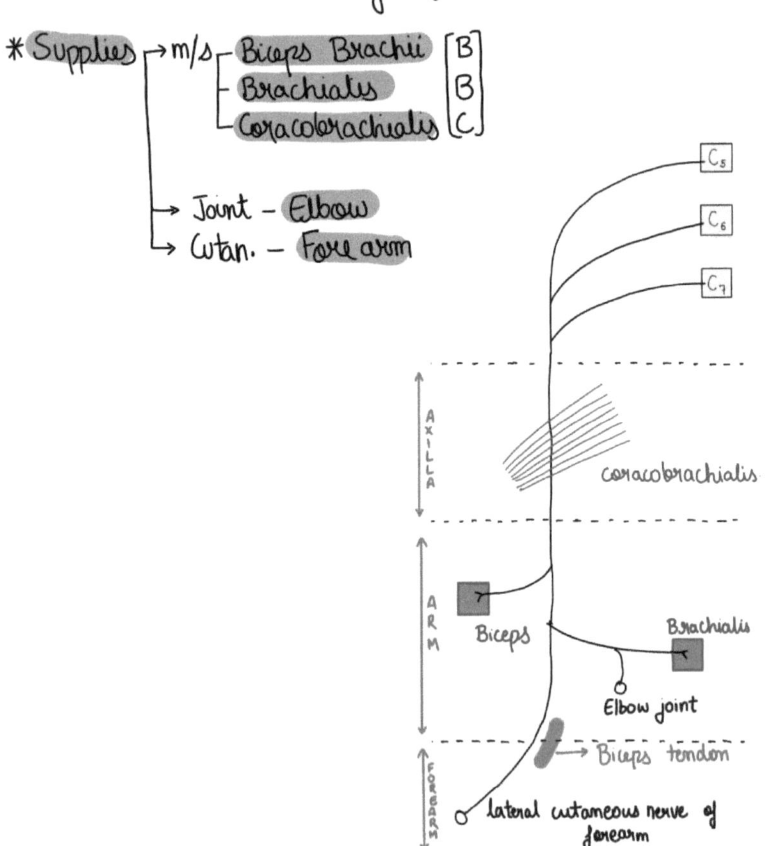

OSTEOLOGY (BONES)

"There is nothing impossible to they who will try."
— Alexander the Great

CLAVICLE

* Introduction
  - It is a S-Shaped bone, lying horzentally at the junction of neck with trunk on the Anterior aspect of body
  - Joints → sternum & I- Rib (Medially)
    ↳ scapula & Acromian Pr. (laterally)

* Anatomical Position & Side determinatⁿ
  - Keep clavicle : horizentally
  - Flattened end : medially
  - Enlarged Quadrilateral end : laterally.
  - Shaft → Med. 2/3 : convex anterior
    ↳ Lat. 1/3 : concave anterior
  - Longitudinal/ Subclavian groove – inferiorly

* Peculiarities
  - only Horz. long Bone
  - 1st bone to Start ossifying (6 WK.) ⟶ Last to complete (25 yr.)
  - No medullary Cavity
  - Medial end – ossifies in cart.] Membranocartilagenous ossification
    Rest – ossifies in memb.

* Attachement ⇒ m/s

origin	insertion
- Deltoid	- Trapezius
- Sternocleidomastoid	- SubClavius
- Pectoralis Major	

⇒ Lig.(s) - Coraco-clavicular
- Costoclavicular
- Inter-clavicular

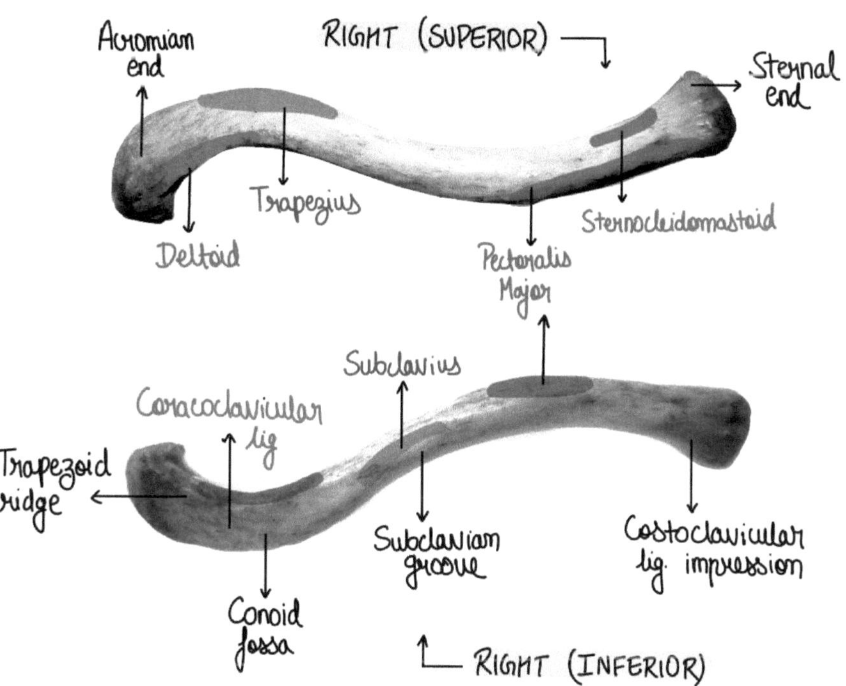

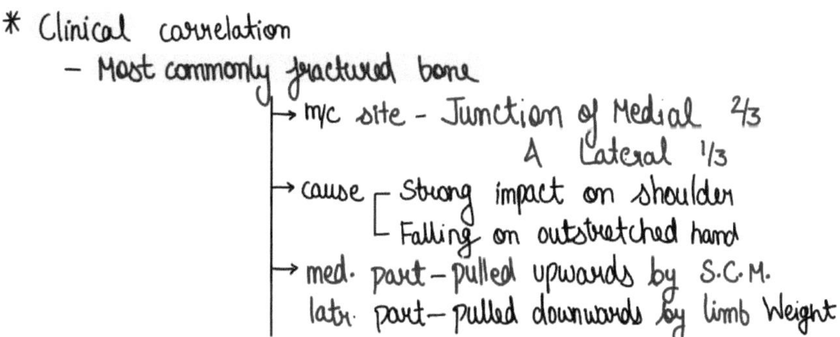

* Clinical correlation

- Most commonly fractured bone
  - → m/c site - Junction of Medial 2/3 & Lateral 1/3
  - → cause
    - Strong impact on shoulder
    - Falling on outstretched hand
  - → med. part – pulled upwards by S.C.M.
    latr. part – pulled downwards by limb weight

SCAPULA (shoulder blade)

* Introduction

- Triangular bone, in the postero-lateral aspect of trunk
- Lies against 2nd to 7th Rib.

* Anatomical Position & Side determinatn

- Coracoid Process - points forward
- Spinous Process - lies posterior.
- Glenoid Cavity - lateral

* Attachment ⇒ m/s

origin	insertion
- long hd. of biceps & triceps	- Pectoralis minor
- Short hd. of biceps & coracobrach.	- Serratus anterior
- Subscapularis	- Trapezius
- Supra & Infra spinatus.	- Levt. scapulae
- Teres Mj. & Mi.	- Rhomboidus → Mj. / → Mi.
- Lattismus dorsi	

⇒ Lig(s)
- Coraco-acromial
- Coraco-clavicular
- Coraco-humeral
- Suprascapular

* Clinical correlation → Sprengel's deformity (congenital high scapula)

- Scapula develops in neck region during IUL & than descend to normal
- Failure in descend cause this abnormality

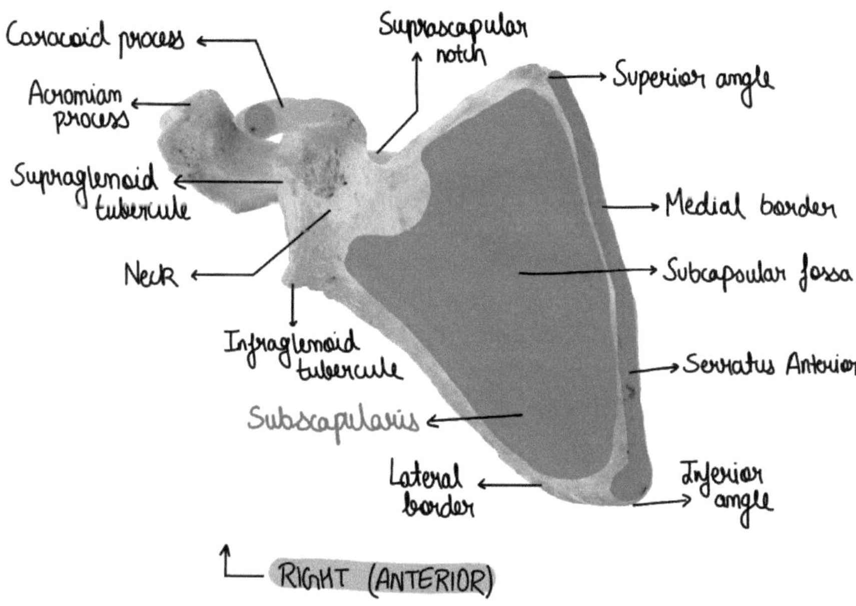
Caracoid process
Suprascapular notch
Superior angle
Acromian process
Supraglenoid tubercule
Medial border
Neck
Subcapoular fossa
Infraglenoid tubercule
Serratus Anterior
Subscapularis
Lateral border
Inferior angle
RIGHT (ANTERIOR)

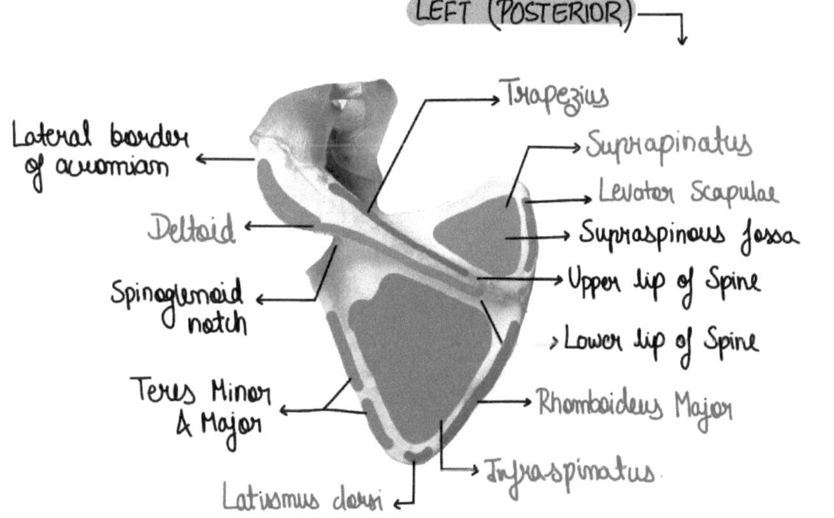
LEFT (POSTERIOR)
Trapezius
Lateral border of acromian
Suprapinatus
Levator Scapulae
Deltoid
Supraspinous fossa
Upper lip of Spine
Spinoglenoid notch
Lower lip of Spine
Teres Minor & Major
Rhomboideus Major
Infraspinatus
Latissmus dorsi

HUMEURS

* Introduction
  - Strongest bone of upper limb.

* Anatomical Position & Side determinatⁿ
  - Rounded head - upwd. & med.
  - Olecranon fossa - lower end
  - Great. + lesser tubercule, Bicipital groove] Anterior
  - Spiral/Radial groove] Posterior

* Attachment ⇒ m/s

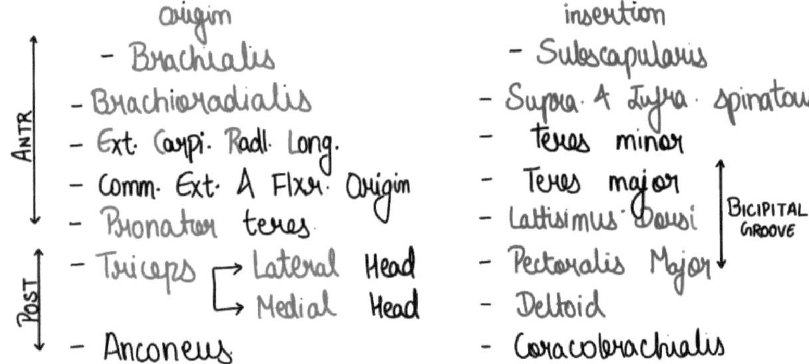

* Clinical correlation
  - Nerves directly related to Humerus
    - → Axillary - around Surgical neck
    - → Radial - radial groove
    - → Ulnar - behind medial epicondyle

  ] involved in fracture

- Common sites of fracture → Shaft, Surgical neck, Supracondylar.

  - caused by fall on outstreched hand
  - show unduly prominent elbow 4 bckwd displacement of lower fragment
  - Brachial artery injury lead to VOLKMAN'S ISCHEMIC CONTRACTURE or MYOSITIS OSSIFICANS

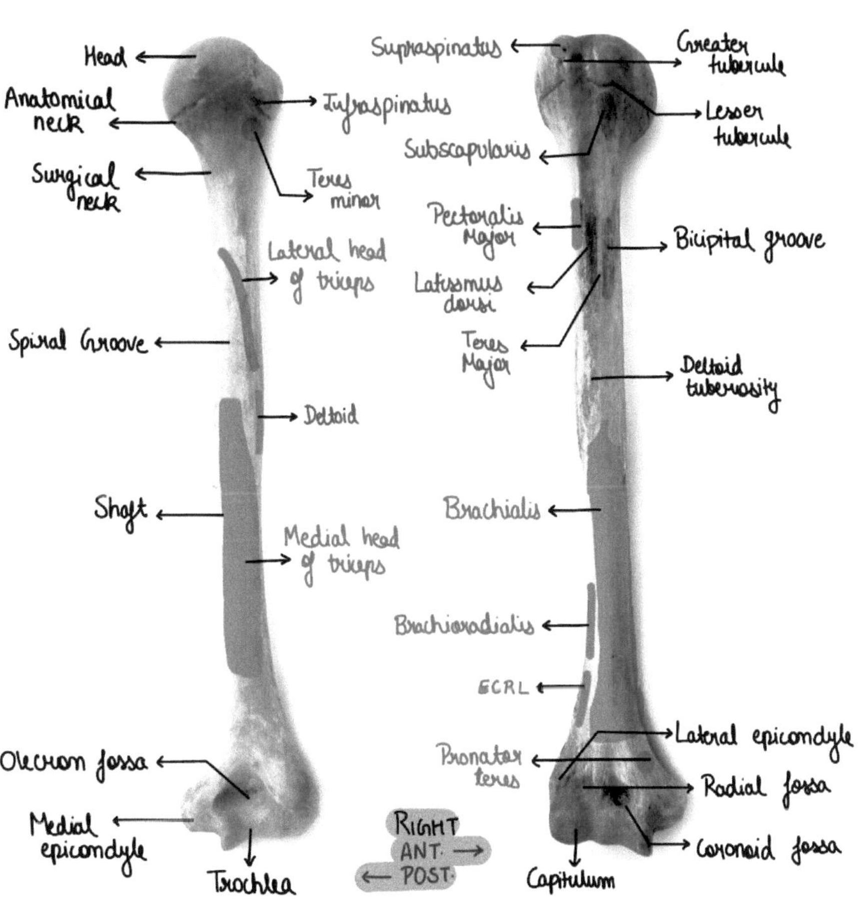

RADIUS & ULNA

Ulna

* Introduction

Medial bone of forearm

- Upper end
  - → 2 Processes – Olecron, Coronoid
  - → 2 notches – Trochlear, Coronoid
- Shaft
  - → 3 borders – Anterior, Posterior, Lateral
  - → 3 surfaces – Anterior, Posterior, Medial
- Lower end → Head, Styloid Process

* Side Determination

- Keep bone vertically in such a way that its hook-like surface upwards
- Concavity of hook & the coronoid process looking forward

* Attachment

- Triceps brachii
- Supinator
- Flexor digitorum superficialis
- Pronator teres
- Flexor digitorum profundus
- Pronator Quadratus
- Flexor Carpi Ulnaris
- Extensor Carpi Ulnaris
- Anconeus

* Ossification

- Shaft & most of upper end of Ulna ossify from 1° centre
- Superior part of olecron process ossify from 2° centre
- Lower end ossifies from 2° secondry

* Clinical
- Ulna is stabilising bone of forearm
- Olecron fractured by fall on elbow tip.

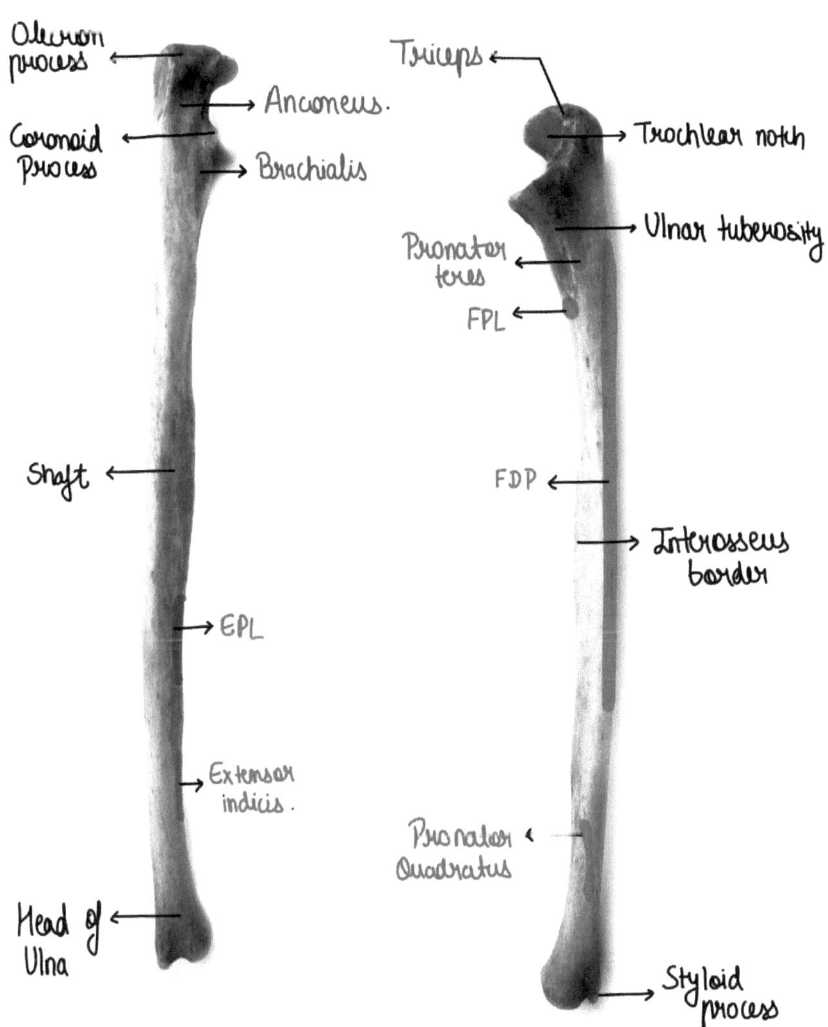

Radius

* Introduction

Lateral bone of forearm.

- Upper end - Head, neck & tuberosity

Shaft → 3 borders - Anterior, Posterior, Medial
→ 3 surfaces - Anterior, Posterior, Lateral.

Lower end - 5 surfaces - Anterior, Posterior, Medial, Lateral, Inferior

* Side Determination
- Place bone vertically, with narrow end upwards
- Styloid Process is located lower end laterally

* Attachment
- Biceps brachii
- Supinator
- Pronator teres
- Brachioradialis
- Radial head of FDS.
- Flexor Pollicis longus
- Pronator Quadratus.

* Ossification
- Shaft from 1° centre, appear during 8th week of IUL
- Upper & Lower end, ossifies from 2° centre, fuse by 18th, 20th year

* Clinical

Colli's Fracture - Fracture 2cm above lower end of Radius

Pulled Elbow - Due to sudden powerful jerk on child hand

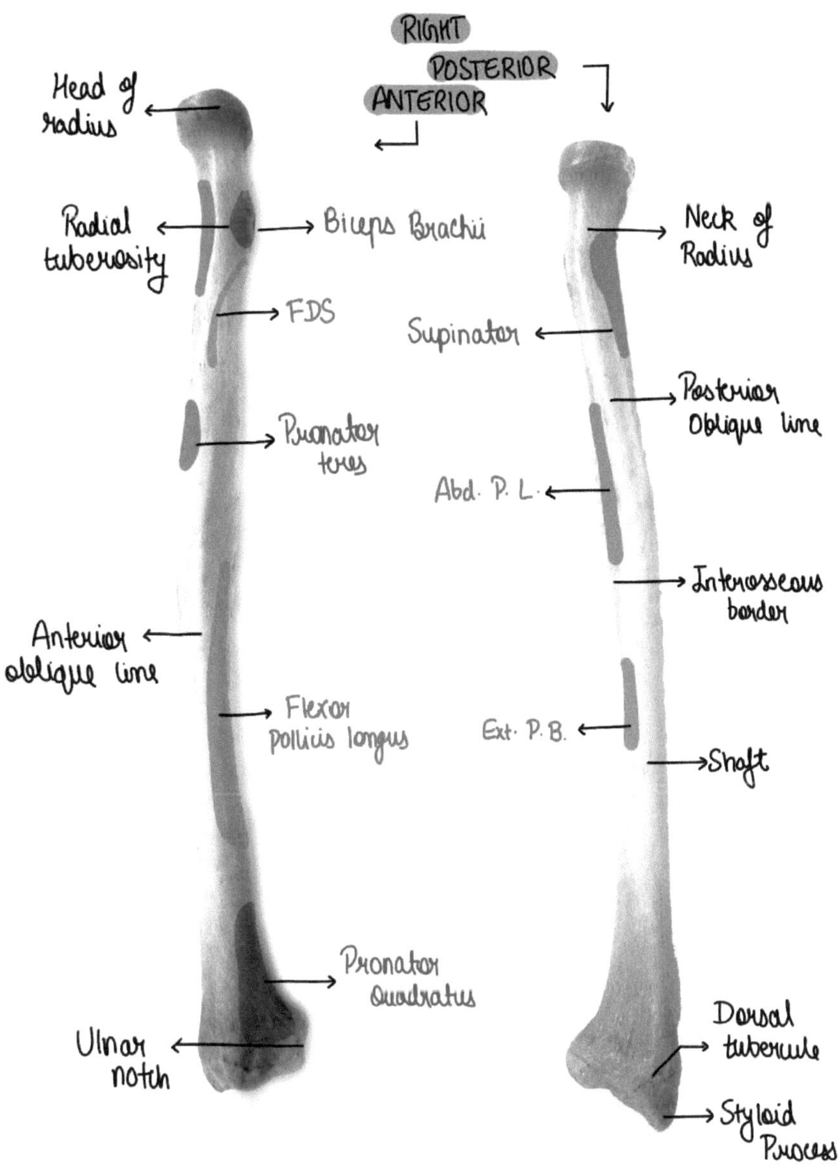
RIGHT
POSTERIOR
ANTERIOR
Head of radius
Radial tuberosity
Biceps Brachii
FDS
Pronator teres
Anterior oblique line
Flexor pollicis longus
Pronator Quadratus
Ulnar notch
Neck of Radius
Supinator
Posterior Oblique line
Abd. P. L.
Interosseous border
Ext. P. B.
Shaft
Dorsal tubercule
Styloid Process

HAND

Carpal Bones

* 8 bones arranged in 2 rows.

	Proximal	Distal	
(boat shape)	- Scaphoid	- Trapezium	
(half moon shape)	- Lunate	- Trapezoid	
(pyramid shape)	- Triquetral	- Capitate	
(pea like)	- Pisiform	- Hamate.	(wedge shaped + Hook)

Ossification- 1st → Capitate - 3 months
last → Pisiform - 12 year.

* Clinical - Fracture of scaphoid is quite common, caused by fall on outstretched hand.
- Dislocation of lunate is also seen

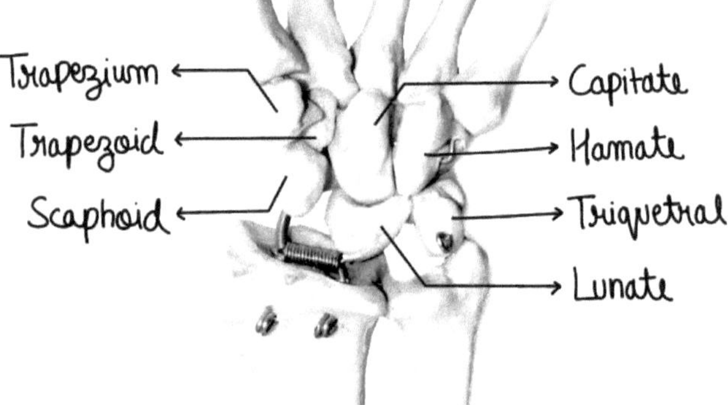

Metacarpal Bones

- 5 miniature long bones (named lateral to medial)
- Head is round, placed distally & has articular surface
- Base is proximal & irregularly expanded
- Shaft is concave on palmar surface
- 1st metacarpal is shortest, it doesn't articulate with any other metacarpal
- 3rd metacarpal have styloid process at base

Ossification

- Shafts ossify from one primary centre each
- 2° centre appear in 2nd to 5th metacarpals

* Clinical

- Bennett's fracture = Fracture of 1st metacarpal base

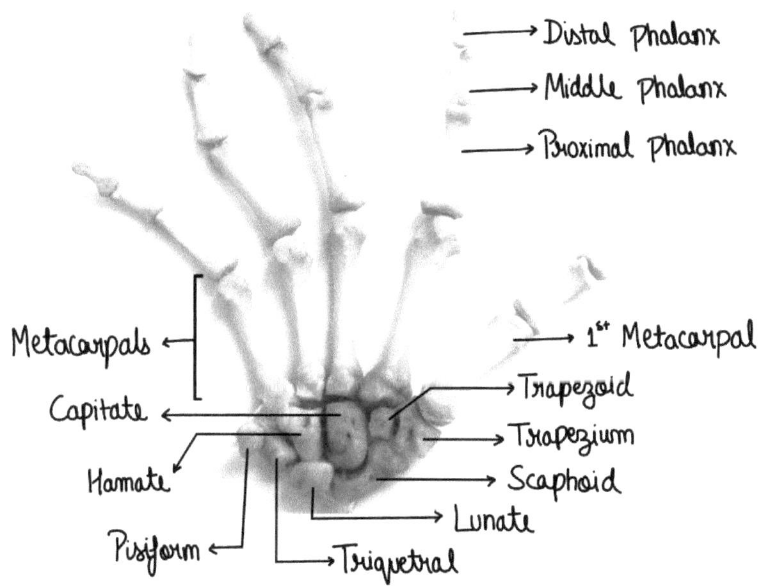

Phalanges

- 14 in each hand (2+3+3+3+3)
- Base → Proximal phal ⇒ concave oval fascet → articulate with head of metacarpal
  → Middle/Distal ⇒ 2 small concave fascet
- Shaft → Tapers towards the head
- Head → Proximal/Middle ⇒ Pulley shaped articular surface
  → Distal ⇒ Not articular; horse shoe shaped tuberosity

Ossification

- 1° centre for shaft, appear first for distal (8th week) than proximal (10th) & last for middle (12th)
- 2° centre appears for base.

* Clinical

- Buddy splint = Splinting of fractured phalynx with adjacent phalynx of normal finger

RADIOLOGY

"Out of the mountain of despair, a stone of hope."
— Martin Luther King, Jr.

RADIOLOGY

Clavicle

Coracoid Process

Acromian Process

Humeral Head

Glenoid

Humerus

Body of Scapula

RIGHT AP View

LEFT OBLIQUE View

Humerus

Lateral epicondyle

Olecron process

Capitulum

Trochlea

Radial head

Radial tubercule

Ulna

Radius

Radius

Ulna

Radial head

Olecron

Capitulum/ Trochlea

RIGHT LATERAL View

RIGHT
MEDIAL

Distal Phl.
Middle Phl.
Proximal Phl.
Metacarpals
Hamate
Capitate
Triquetral
Trapezium
Pisiform
Trapezoid
Lumate
Scaphoid

SURFACE MARKING

" Believe in yourself and keep your standards high, life wants to give you what you want "

SURFACE MARKING

Major Veins

Cephalic - A - Deltopectoral groove (below coracoid branch)
B - at front of elbow in between Biceps tendon and brachioradialis muscle

Basilic - C - Humerus (mid shaft)
D - Medial side of medial epicondyle

Palmar Arches

Superficial Palmar arch - A - Lateral to pisiform
- B - Medial to hook of Hamate
- C - Centre of Palm
- D - Distal border of thenar eminence

Deep Palmar arch - E - Just distal to hook of hamate
- F - 1st Intermetacarpal space (Proximal)

Major Artries

A - Mid Point Clavicle
B - Lower end of lateral wall
C - Neck of Radius.
D - Site of Radial Pulse
E - Lateral to pisiform bone

AB - Axillary artery
BC - Brachial artery
CD - Radial artery
CE - Ulnar artery

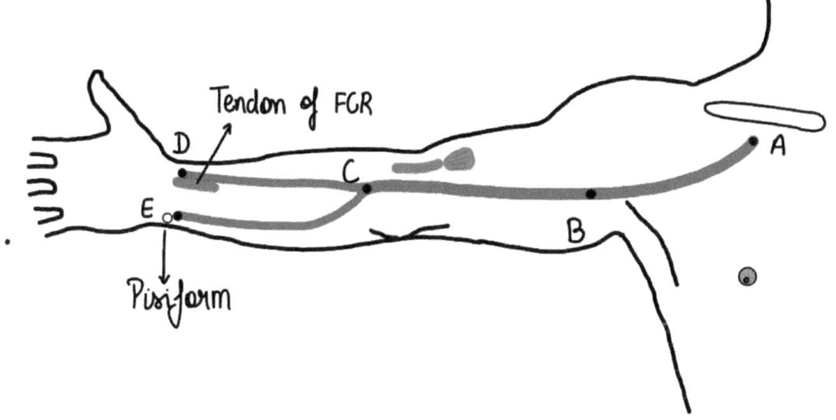

Printed by Libri Plureos GmbH in Hamburg,
Germany